What Do We Know About Comparing Ma

Everything is made out of materials. There are many different types of material. We learn about materials by looking closely at them and feeling them.

1 **How many different materials can you see in this diagram?**

2 **Choose two different materials you can find in your bedroom. Record how each one looks and feels.**

Two different materials can have both similar and different properties.

3 **Name another material that looks or feels similar to one of your choices. Explain your choice.**

Describing and Comparing Materials

Describing materials

Word box
compare
describe
property

Some different materials.

There are eight different materials in this diagram. We **describe** materials by observing them closely. We can see how they look by looking at the diagram but we cannot describe how they feel. We need to touch them to do that.

Look and feel

You will need: the materials in the diagram

1 Observe them closely by looking at and feeling them.

2 List the different materials.

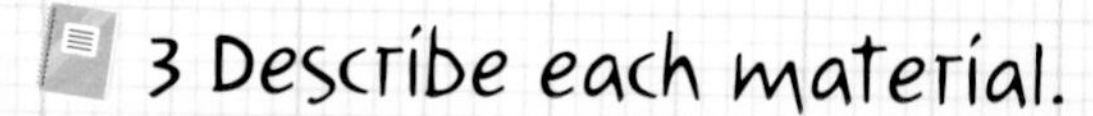

3 Describe each material.

Comparing materials

When we **compare** materials we say how their **properties** are similar and different. We compare materials to find things with a similar property.

These objects all have a similar property.

1a What is the similar property of these objects?

1b What else could you add to this collection?

2a What would you put in a collection of sharp objects?

2b Name something that could *not* go in that collection? Why?

3a What objects could you put in a collection of flexible things?

3b Name something that could *not* go in that collection? Why?

Exploring Soft Materials

Word box
hard
soft

Toys made out of **soft** materials squash and bend so do not hurt us when we cuddle them. Toys made out of **hard** materials do not squash and bend. They can hurt if we cuddle them.

1a Which toys in the picture would be nice to cuddle?

1b Why would they be nice to cuddle?

2a Which toys in the picture would *not* be nice to cuddle?

2b Why would they not be nice to cuddle?

3 Draw and label some soft and hard toys of your own.

Soft toys can be stuffed with different types of stuffing to help make them soft. In the past the only stuffing that was used was sawdust.

Polyester fluff, polystyrene balls and tissue paper are all different types of stuffing.

Sawdust

Comparing stuffing

You will need: sawdust, polyester fluff, polystyrene balls

Work in a small group and compare these different types of stuffing.

1 Which do you think is the best type of stuffing to stuff a soft toy?

2 Why have you chosen this type of stuffing?

Comparing Old and Modern Teddy Bears

The first teddy bears were made over 100 years ago. They were made very differently then. They were stuffed with sawdust.

The first bears were made from soft fur called mohair.

The first bears had black leather eyes.

A modern teddy bear is not made from these materials. 'Modern' means it is made now.

Making modern teddy bears

1 With a partner find out how teddy bears are made today.

2 Make an information page for a modern bear. Write and draw pictures to show how a modern teddy bear is made.

Look at these pictures of teddy bear eyes:

Leather

Glass

Plastic

1 What are the differences between these eyes?

2a Which do you think is the best material to use to make teddy bear eyes?

2b Why have you chosen this material?

The outside of a modern teddy bear is not always fur.

Research modern teddy bears

1 With a partner look for pictures and find out about different types of modern teddy bears.

2 Draw and write about the teddy bear you like best.

Make a Sock Creature

Make a sock puppet

You will need: scissors, glue, different types of stuffing, coloured felt, coloured wool, a sock, stick-on eyes

Use the equipment listed to design your creature.

1 Stick eyes onto your sock creature.

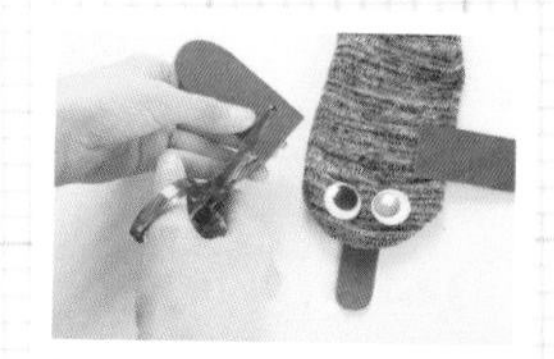

2 Cut out a felt mouth, nose and ears. Stick them on to finish the face.

3 Stick on wool for hair and add felt legs.

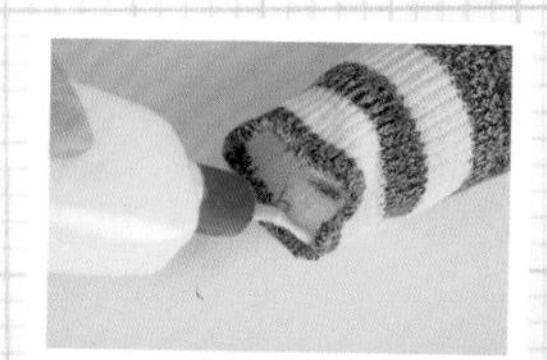

4 Choose some stuffing and stuff the sock.

5 Glue the open end of the sock together.

Science Skills

Classify it!

Word box
classify

When we **classify** things we sort them into groups. All the things in any group will have something similar about them. Two ways we can sort things are:

- into two groups using opposites
- into two groups of objects that
  - have a property
  - do not have a property.

1 Which dolls are soft and which are not soft?

Wooden doll

Plastic doll

Knitted doll

Rag doll

China doll

Exploring Slime

Different novelty slimes.

There are different types of slime. Some of their properties are similar. In other ways they can be different.

Comparing slimes

You will need: different types of slime

1 Work in a small group to observe the different slimes. Discuss their properties.

2a Choose one of the slimes. Describe its properties in three words.

2b Choose another type of slime. How is it similar to your first choice?

2c How is it different?

A ball of cornflour slime.

Cornflour slime after 5 minutes.

These diagrams show cornflour slime left on a saucer in a warm classroom for a week.

Cornflour slime after a week.

1 Describe the changes to a partner.

Changing slimes

You will need: different types of slime, two saucers

1 Work in a small group. Choose one thick sticky slime and one thin runny slime.

2 Try to roll them into similar-sized small balls.

3 Place each one on a saucer.

4 Leave them for a week. How did they change?

Investigate it!

Word box
float
sink

Sometimes when we put things in water they **sink**. This means they fall to the bottom of the water. Other things **float**. This means they stay on the top of the water.

Look at this duck in a stream.

1 What is floating in the diagram?

2 What has sunk in the diagram?

Some children investigated whether all types of paper sink. They crumpled up small pieces of paper. They put them in a bowl of water. They counted how long before each piece started to sink.

This is their table.

Type of paper	Number counted to before the paper started to sink
Kitchen roll	5
Tissue	Floated
Toilet paper	2
Paper towel	15

This is what the children thought.

The toilet paper sank quickest.

All the papers sank.

The paper towel sank slowest.

Kitchen roll will be best for a toy boat.

3 Look at the table. Are the children right? Explain your answers.

Transparent, Opaque or Translucent?

Transparent materials let light through.

Opaque materials do not let light through.

Translucent materials let just a little bit of light through.

Word box
opaque
translucent
transparent

Cling film

Metal foil

Greaseproof paper

Transparent, translucent or opaque?

You will need: 10 cm square pieces of cling film, metal foil and greaseproof paper

1 Which material is transparent, which is translucent, and which is opaque?

2 List two other materials you think are transparent, two you think are translucent and two you think are opaque.

An easy way to test for transparency is to place a piece of material over a torch that is switched on.

1 What will you see if the material is transparent?
2 What will you see if the material is opaque?
3 What will you see if the material is translucent?

Can light pass through?

You will need: a torch, 10 cm square pieces of cling film, metal foil and greaseproof paper, the six materials you listed in the last activity

Work in a small group.

1 Use the torch to find out which materials are transparent, translucent and opaque.

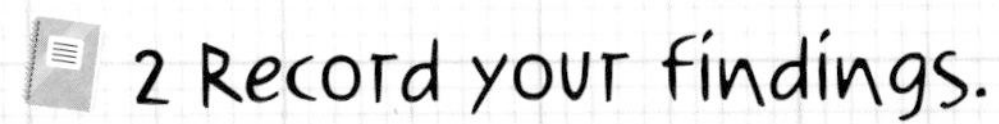

2 Record your findings.

Glossary

Classify sort into groups, put similar things together

Compare look at how things are similar and different

Describe say what something is like

Float to stay on top of the surface of water

Hard does not squash and bend, not nice to cuddle

Opaque does not let light through

Property look and feel of an object/material

Sink to drop through water to the bottom

Soft squashes and bends, nice to cuddle

Translucent lets some light through

Transparent lets light through